Get Your
FINANCIALDUCKS
in a Row

GREGORYGENTRY
CEP, RFC

Get Your
FINANCIAL DUCKS
in a Row

GREGORY GENTRY
CEP, RFC

Advantage

Published by Advantage, Charleston, South Carolina.
Member of Advantage Media Group.

ADVANTAGE is a registered trademark and the Advantage colophon is a trademark of Advantage Media Group, Inc.

Printed in the United States of America.

ISBN: 978-159932-496-8
LCCN: 2014938308

Book design by George Stevens.

This publication is designed to provide accurate and authoritative information in regard to the subject matter covered. It is sold with the understanding that the publisher is not engaged in rendering legal, accounting, or other professional services. If legal advice or other expert assistance is required, the services of a competent professional person should be sought.

Advantage Media Group is proud to be a part of the Tree Neutral® program. Tree Neutral offsets the number of trees consumed in the production and printing of this book by taking proactive steps such as planting trees in direct proportion to the number of trees used to print books. To learn more about Tree Neutral, please visit www.treeneutral.com. To learn more about Advantage's commitment to being a responsible steward of the environment, please visit www.advantagefamily.com/green

Advantage Media Group is a publisher of business, self-improvement, and professional development books and online learning. We help entrepreneurs, business leaders, and professionals share their Stories, Passion, and Knowledge to help others Learn & Grow. Do you have a manuscript or book idea that you would like us to consider for publishing? Please visit advantagefamily.com or call 1.866.775.1696.

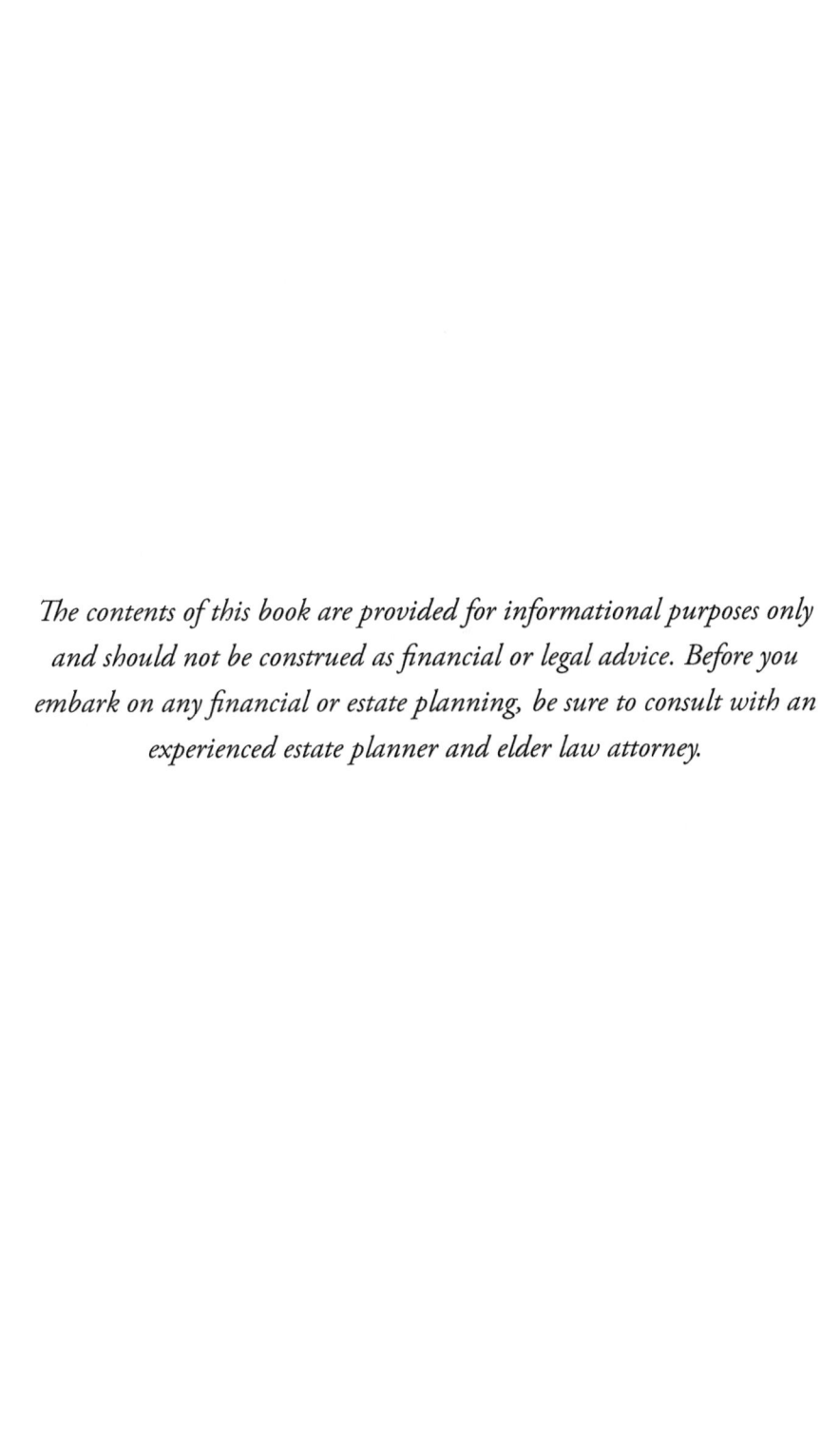

🦆 | CONTENTS

🦆 | INTRODUCTION

What's the Big Deal about Having a Plan?

I started as a financial planner in 1981, selling term life insurance and mutual funds. I sold term insurance because term gave young families the largest guaranteed death benefit and mutual funds would allow young families to invest as little as $25 a month in one of the biggest bull markets in history. The combination really gave young families the biggest "bang for the buck."

After a few years in the business, I realized that even though I was making a difference in young family's lives, my clients did not have a financial plan that would serve them for life. For less money, I was providing four or five times as much term life insurance coverage when the kids were young and the need was great. Mutual funds really captured the public's attention in the 1980s and 1990s when mutual fund investment hit record highs and investors saw incredible returns. But the more I brought on board clients who were older and close to retirement age, the more I realized the big name companies I worked for weren't concerned about clients having a real plan. I was just helping clients save money for retirement and when they reached retirement, they were on their own.

There was no training on any of the different forms of ownership that were available to clients or which one was best under different circumstances. I was taught to make the spouse the first beneficiary and kids contingent (secondary) beneficiaries without even thinking about the fact that a probate judge would not allow a minor to receive a large life insurance settlement.

I decided that I needed to find out everything on my own if my clients were going to have a true retirement plan and be given real choices.

The light came on when a friend of mine lost his mother and asked me to help him with her estate. He had lost his father several years before, but he knew his parents had a well-known attorney, insurance agent and a broker in the town where they lived, and he was sure everything was in order. I actually knew all three of the professionals his parents used, and because they were well known, I thought helping my friend would be a great learning opportunity for me. I was right. It was truly a learning experience and over the next several months, I really got an education. My friend's parents had accumulated a large estate and at the time, the federal estate tax exemption was $325,000, meaning everything over that amount could be taxed up to 55 percent. The son had called the family attorney when his mother was very ill to see if there was anything he needed to do. He was told the will had recently been updated after his father's death and everything was in order. The family insurance agent knew my friend's parents would have state and federal estate taxes to pay, so he had sold them each a large life

> *The light came on when a friend of mine lost his mother and asked me to help him with her estate.*

insurance policy to help cover the cost of the estate taxes. After the father's death, the broker had explained to the mother that she could start transferring shares of stock to her son to avoid some of the estate taxes that were inevitable.

Even though the will was in order and had been updated, what we realized too late was that the attorney had not written and funded a living trust. If he had done so, both parents could have kept their $325,000 federal estate tax exemption and saved a small fortune in estate taxes, not to mention the 6 percent the attorney ended up charging for probate.

The insurance agent had written a separate life insurance policy for each parent. Since the parents owned their own policies, they had what are called incidents of ownership, which caused two bad things to happen. When the father died, the mother received a death claim check (to be used to pay death taxes), which the mother put into an investment account. At her death, this account actually increased her estate size, creating more taxes due! When the mother died, since she owned her policy, she had also had an "incident of ownership" and her insurance was included in her estate tax calculation.

The broker, in gifting the stocks to the son, had transferred the mother's tax basis (the value she had paid for the stocks years earlier) to the son. This meant that even though the stocks avoided probate, the son would now pay a capital gains tax on the value above the mother's calculated tax basis when the stocks were sold. If the broker had left the stocks in the mother's name, they would have received a step-up in basis (forgiveness) of capital gains tax and a stock sale would have been tax-free to the son. Unfortunately, even though the stocks did not have to go through probate, since the gifts occurred within three years of the mother's death, the value was brought back into the estate for the estate tax calculation.

When we were trying to figure all this out, we paid several visits to the family tax preparer, who told us he had wondered why the parents had done some of the things they had done because he knew it would cost them more in taxes at death. When we asked him why he had not warned the parents, he said, "They didn't ask me."

When I saw what professionals not working together as a team and working outside their expertise had done to my friend, my practice would never be the same. I realized that it really did not make any difference how much money I made for my clients if nothing was in place to help them keep it. The financial cost to my friend was well over $300,000, but the frustrations and delays took just as high a toll. This really drives home the point that it's not what you make that counts; it's what you keep. You want to keep it? Get a plan.

My purpose in writing this book is not to go into detail about all the things you could or should be doing. It's simply to let you know you have choices. There are real options that can bring great rewards to your family. The hard part is finding someone or a team of professionals who are willing to step out of the mold and take the time to tell you and your family what these options are. A knowledgeable financial and estate planner is a great start, followed by an experienced estate planning attorney and tax professional.

🦆 | CHAPTER 1

Getting Started

Is It Time to Call a Family Meeting?

There are many ways a family can put a plan together. To give you an example of one way, let me describe the structure I use the most. I have used what I call the family meeting for almost 30 years very effectively. The family meeting allows you to involve your grown children in your estate planning process if you want to. They can start to understand what your wishes and desires really are as you outline what you want your estate to do for your family in the future. You are in charge, not the kids. Sure, they can share input, but the decisions to be made are yours. Working with a good estate planner during this process is like working with a good coach or trainer. You are paying that professional to coach and guide you, so it's important to have someone you are 100 percent comfortable with. Don't just pick the first person you talk with. Interview that person for the job!

First Things First

The first time I meet with my clients, we are alone so I can openly gather all the facts and numbers needed to put a plan together and I am free from emotional interference to talk with my clients about their kids and grandkids. My clients can speak openly about the kids who are savers or spenders, or maybe about the kids who are married to a spouse my clients can't stand. There might be an emotional or physical issue that I, as an estate planner, really need to know about, including issues that have caused conflict or hard feelings between kids. These are fact-finding meetings that help me find out how the family functions. During these meetings, I help my clients decide whether they are interested in just passing on an inheritance or creating a family legacy. It amazes me how many people have never thought about the difference between the two. What I want to know up front is whether my clients want their kids to get new motorcycles and pool tables, or whether they want to help their kids add to their own retirement funds and/or create a fund to send the grandkids and great-grandkids to college. Do they have a plan? Do they want a plan?

The Truth and Nothing but the Truth

I've always been more interested in telling clients what they need to hear, not what they want to hear, as most financial people do today. You have to remember financial people are salespeople in one form or another. They make a living by selling you things and most of them will sell you things by telling you what you want to hear. Remember, there is a great difference in being sold something and buying something. Having a great plan can really decide the direction your family will take when you are not around anymore. I will always give clients my honest opinion. I often tell clients, "If you were my parents, here is what I would tell you, and I am very serious. I might not be the best at everything, but I am a great listener and it is important that your advisor be one too. Someone who does all the talking is not listening to what is important to you. It is extremely important to have a relationship with an estate planner who is not afraid to tell you the truth. If you don't have this real relationship, you just have someone "selling" you something!

> *A man can be judged by how he treats someone who can do him no good.*

Deciding the type of investment or estate planning tools to use, such as a trust, or what tax strategy to follow is the easy part. It's the succession planning combined with the emotional decisions that have to be made that are hard for most people.

Emotions get in the way of reason. After a couple of meetings, I know what is most important to clients, based on what they have told me, and I know what assets I'll be working with and how we can address the best way to take care of those concerns, no guessing. From the conversations about the kids and grandkids, the plan for the future starts to take shape.

Don't I Have to Treat All the Kids the Same?

If you have two or more kids, I'm betting on the fact one of them (or their spouse) can't handle money and spends everything he or she makes. A recent survey shows 57 percent of adults 19 to 29 years of age are at least partially dependent on their parents to pay their basic bills. I see this all the time: the parents live in a modest, ranch-style home, with 10-year-old cars parked in the driveway, while they give their kids money to pay for those kids' leased BMW parked in front of their $300,000 home, *because the kids spent too much money on their beach vacation.* This is a big concern for parents and really needs to be addressed; most parents just don't know how to deal with it. Kids today think they should be starting out in life with all the nice things their parents took 25 years to accumulate. If your kids are spenders, how are they ever going to be able to help their own kids out as you helped them out?

Everyone needs help sometimes, especially in today's financial environment, and it's only going to get worse. If this describes one (or more) of your kids, get it out in the open and deal with it. Don't think it's going to get better; odds are it won't. I have had clients aged over 90 come into the office wanting to discuss estate plans that pay the estate proceeds to kids over a period of years because the kids spend everything they get, and the kids are in their 70s!

> *The happiest people don't have the best of everything; they just make the best of everything.*

Okay, How Do I Deal with My Big Spender?

There are many, many options. You can distribute interest only over a certain period or make equal distributions over a set period of years. Another option is to give this child half of what you intended to give over a period of time, which acts like speed bumps. Then allocate the other half of the share to this child's kids, your grandkids, for their future health, education, welfare and maintenance needs. This obviously helps your grandkids and takes pressure off your kids down the road so you're not taking away from your kids. Stop and think about how hard you worked for your money and all the things you did without early on. Money left to kids in certain kinds of trusts will actually protect the money left to them from divorces, lawsuits, medical bills, even nursing homes! It's not about trying to treat all your kids the same or being fair; it's about doing the right thing. That's what's fair. You don't have to treat everyone the same, because they are not! Sometimes you protect your kids from themselves. To me, it's not fair to knowingly have one child who has carefully planned, saved money for retirement, and saved money for his or her kid's future education and not protect your other grandkids from the problems caused by a child who has not planned or saved a dime. I will never forget being told, years ago, that the only difference between a bum and an elderly gentleman is money.

Bringing all these concerns out in the open and really addressing them will start to release stress you have had for years. I promise. Throwing your hands up in the air and just letting your kids blow it is not an option a good estate planner is going to give you. It makes more sense to give everything to your grandkids' education or to a great charity that you love than let your kids blow everything. Don't even start me on giving everything to nieces and nephews who live out of state, haven't visited you in 15 years, and don't even care enough to go to your funeral.

So, after the distribution plans start to take shape and you are comfortable with them, it's time for the next meeting, at which I share with the adult kids and their spouses the parent's wishes and desires and how we plan to make those dreams become a reality. We don't share numbers or investment options or who will play key roles in the administration of the plan at the first family meeting. We introduce the family legacy (don't just blow everything) idea. After the kids are introduced to the family legacy idea, we can talk with each child about his or her role. Trust me. Having your will read, after your death, in a dark library, with everyone sitting on the edge of their chairs, only belongs in the movies.

Picking the Right People to Be in Charge

This is a big deal. The majority of people want to have all their kids serve equally as investment advisor, executor, trustee, or power of attorney. What a mistake. Why would you force the person who really will be there for you to work with a sibling or other family member who couldn't care less and doesn't want any responsibility? Don't make this hard. Who is going to be the one who will take you to the doctor when you're sick and will take you shopping or do your shopping for you, clean your house, write your checks and pay your bills when you can't? This is the person who should take charge. However, that person also needs to be a strong person who will not let a sibling or family member step in and bully him or her. One of my clients lost her husband and had a less than desirable relationship with her two kids who lived hours away and seldom saw her. After much thought she decided to have her much-loved sister serve as her power of attorney and trustee of her estate. She was afraid her kids, who would go for long periods of time without even talking to each other, would fight and squabble over her assets when she was gone. The sisters, who lived in the same town, were together constantly, as close as two sisters could be. After a couple of years, the client started to become very forgetful, to the point, I believe without doubt, she was incompetent to make financial decisions. The kids were under the belief their mother had been left a large sum of money by their stepfather. So, one day, one of the kids called their aunt (their mother's sister) and told her the siblings had talked and believed they should step in and move their mother out of state to be closer to one of them. She would be hours from her sister, her friends, her church, and of course, the siblings would now be in charge of her money.

Here is the problem: they told the sister who had the power of attorney that she had to promise to not tell their mother, as they did not want to upset her, and instead of standing her ground, the mother's sister allowed herself to be bullied into agreeing with the children. You can imagine how this turned out. The kids came to town, cleaned out the mother's bank accounts, loaded her apartment up in a U-Haul, and left the state in the middle of the night. The client had done everything right but had picked the wrong person to be in charge. This simple problem could have been easily avoided, but it turned into a runaway train wreck. You have to be able to separate emotions from reality and carefully put in charge the people who will get the job done. Maybe it would be your oldest child, but it might be the youngest. After all these considerations and issues, you're ready to put a plan in place—your plan, not your kids' plan.

Getting Your Ducks in a Row

1. *Design your plan based on your wishes and desires, not someone else's.*

2. *You do not have to treat everyone the same.*

3. *Take time to pick the right family member or friend to be in charge*

🦆 | CHAPTER 2

The Health Care Crisis and Medicare

Without doubt, the biggest fear I have for my clients is the looming health care crisis and my clients' total unawareness of what is going to happen. Let's start with Medicare and what it will and won't do for you. The lack of knowledge on this issue is not limited by people's levels of income or education even though the issue really is straightforward. Medicare is health insurance for people age 65 and older, or under age 65 if they have certain disabilities, or any age if they have renal disease (permanent kidney failure). The program was started in 1965 and was created to help pay for doctors, medical expenses and hospitalization for disabled and elderly people.

Medicare has two major parts, known as Part A and Part B, and two secondary parts, known as Part C and Part D. Part A, which is often referred to as hospital insurance, pays part of inpatient hospital care, skilled nursing care, hospice and other services. Part B, often called medical insurance, helps pay doctor's fees, outpatient hospital visits and other medical services and supplies. Part C, which is known as Medicare Advantage, allows you to choose to receive all your healthcare services through a provider organization such as an

HMO or PPO. Medicare Part D, which covers prescription drugs, offers enrollment in prescription drug plans that can lower the cost of prescriptions.

Medicare does not pay for your custodial nursing home care or nonrehabilitation care. It is amazing how many people really believe Medicare will cover most costs of a nursing home stay. Medicare will pay for 20 days if you come from a three-day hospital stay and can pay for up to 100 days, maximum, depending on where you go and what kind of care you need and how many hoops you can jump through. If the care needed is skilled, not custodial, which is what most people need in a nursing home, and you are able and willing to undergo therapy, you can apply for the extra days. These extra days can stop anytime you're not able to jump through the hoops. The biggest nursing home fear for most of us is Alzheimer's disease. It is a degenerative disorder for which skilled care is not an option because Medicare sees rehabilitation to be of little help.

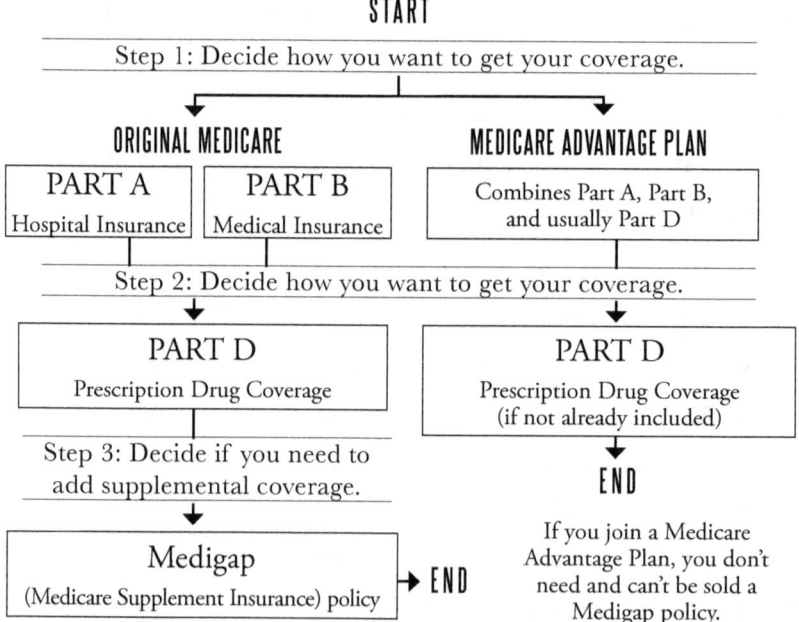

START

Step 1: Decide how you want to get your coverage.

ORIGINAL MEDICARE		MEDICARE ADVANTAGE PLAN
PART A Hospital Insurance	**PART B** Medical Insurance	Combines Part A, Part B, and usually Part D

Step 2: Decide how you want to get your coverage.

PART D Prescription Drug Coverage	PART D Prescription Drug Coverage (if not already included)

Step 3: Decide if you need to add supplemental coverage.

END

Medigap (Medicare Supplement Insurance) policy → **END**

If you join a Medicare Advantage Plan, you don't need and can't be sold a Medigap policy.

Medicare Supplement or Gap Insurance

While most people are familiar with Original Medicare, some may not be aware that Medicare still requires you to pay for a number of uncovered expenses such as deductibles, copayments and coinsurance. Therefore, even though Medicare Parts A and B potentially provide good coverage for your health care and hospitalization needs, the program still leaves a number of "gaps" in terms of members' out-of-pocket costs. In fact, although the coverage provided by Medicare is affordable (you're paying for it), it tends to cover only 80 percent of your medical expenses. In many cases these uncovered charges (e.g., deductibles, copays, prescriptions and other expenses) can really add up, potentially causing financial hardship. This is where Medicare supplemental insurance, oftentimes referred to as Medigap coverage, comes in. These plans are designed to fill in the "gaps" that are left by Medicare's benefits, potentially saving you thousands of dollars per year.

Medicare Advantage Plans

A Medicare Advantage plan is a type of Medicare health plan offered by a private company that contracts with Medicare to provide you with all your Part A and Part B benefits. Medicare Advantage plans include health maintenance organizations, preferred provider organizations, private fee-for-service plans, special needs plans, and Medicare medical savings account plans. If you're enrolled in a Medicare Advantage plan, Medicare services are covered through the plan and aren't paid for under Original Medicare. Most Medicare Advantage plans offer prescription drug coverage. Medicare Advantage plans, sometimes called Part C or MA plans, are offered by private companies approved by Medicare. If you enroll in a Medicare Advantage plan, you still have Medicare. You'll get your Medicare Part A (hospital insurance) and Medicare Part B (medical insurance) coverage from the Medicare Advantage plan and not Original Medicare.

Get Your Ducks in a Row

1. *Medicare Part A is often referred to as hospital insurance.*

2. *Medicare Part B is often referred to as medical insurance.*

3. *Medicare supplement policies fill in the gap.*

🦆 | CHAPTER 3

The Medicaid Maze

If you have not planned for your long-term care you will probably find yourself in the Medicaid maze at some point in the future. Medicaid is a federal program that is administered at the state level and can help you pay for nursing home care. To add to the confusion, each county in the state can have its own interpretation of the code. I have seen that firsthand many times. If you do not have the funds to pay for a nursing home stay, you will be directed by the nursing home to talk to Medicaid to see if you qualify for Medicaid coverage. They will even set your appointment up for you because they want to be paid. Medicaid has three basic eligibility tests to see if you qualify. The Category test makes sure you are at least 65 years old, blind or disabled. The Income test determines how much income you will need to spend down, and the Asset test determines how much of your assets you get to keep. In most states, if you are single, the limit is $2,000 and if you are married, you get to keep up to $109,560. You can easily find yourself too rich to be poor and too poor to be rich, all at the same time. If you are caught in a situation in which Medicaid would be your only way to pay for long-term care, the more important question may not be what you get to keep as much as what you get to keep using during your lifetime.

What You Can Keep or Use

If a sick spouse goes into a nursing home, the spouse who does not need nursing home care can take advantage of some assets that are exempt from the required Medicaid spend-down. He or she can continue to live at home without the fear of having to sell the property during the couple's lifetime. The same can apply to a single person if that person receives qualified, in-home, custodial care. In most states, for a home to be considered exempt, there is a $500,000 limit on its value.

The spouse living independently can keep one reasonably valued vehicle if it is used to provide transportation and can keep a life insurance policy if the cash value (savings) does not exceed $1,500. In most states, a funeral trust can be purchased to shelter up to $12,500 in cash to pay for a funeral. Medicaid will usually exempt most personal property unless it includes collectables, expensive art or antiques. The independent spouse can use these items. There is a big difference between using and keeping.

If you qualify for Medicaid, it will be made clear that you are "using" these assets: They are no longer yours to do whatever you want to with and a review will be made from time to time to make sure you have not tried to give the assets away or sell them. Medicaid has a State Recovery Program to recover assets at the second spouse's death to reimburse the agency for funds it spent on nursing home care. That is why Medicaid does not permit the sale or donation of assets after a prospective nursing home patient has qualified for Medicaid coverage.

I had a top Medicaid official tell a small group of people I was with earlier this year that there is a big misconception that Medicaid will take a couple's house after the second spouse dies if that spouse died owing funds to Medicaid. The Medicaid official said, "We won't take your parents' home! Now, we might make you sell it to come up with the cash to pay us back, but we will never take it." Unbelievable. He somehow thought that would make people feel better about losing Mom and Dad's house. The same gentleman said over and over that Medicaid is not an entitlement program; it is a health care loan that needs to be paid back. I guess that put things in perspective.

> *Medicaid is not an entitlement program; it is a health care loan that needs to be paid back.*

There is a 60-month, gifting, look-back period, that begins when your Medicaid application is filed and looks back to prevent you from simply giving your assets to your kids and then immediately applying for coverage. So any asset protection planning can't be done in the ambulance going to the nursing home from the hospital. Even though I have actually gotten some of those calls, your options are limited to say the least.

There is a penalty period that Medicaid applies to any asset gifted within the 60-month, look-back period, and sometimes the penalty can actually work in your favor if you have a good planner or elder attorney to guide you. Most states offer what is called a penalty divisor: approximately $5,000. The divisor is a simple calculation designed to tell you how long you have to wait before applying for Medicaid if you have given gifts during the 60-month look back. If you give $100,000 away during the look-back period, Medicaid divides the gift ($100,000) by the $5,000 divisor, which, in this case, means you are not allowed to apply for Medicaid for 20 months.

I had a client who had saved all her life to help send her only grandchild to college. No one in the family had ever gone to college, so it was a big deal. For years and years this lady saved everything she could. Her husband had died years before and she had gone without many things she would like to have had. The day came when her granddaughter was off to college and, as promised, the grandmother started paying the bills. For the next four years she was able to pay the majority of the tuition. The day came when she watched her granddaughter walk across the stage and receive her diploma. Grandma was the proudest person in the audience. Three months after she watched her granddaughter walk across that stage, she had a massive stoke. She spent two weeks in the hospital and then was taken to a nursing home. When the Medicaid specialist took her application, she, of course, was asked if she had given any assets away in the previous 60 months. Of course,

The tax gifting allowance means you are allowed to "gift" $14,000 a year to anyone, but that is not a Medicaid gifting allowance.

she did not qualify for Medicaid and lost everything she had left. The tax gifting allowance means you are allowed to "gift" $14,000 a year to anyone, but that is *not* a Medicaid gifting allowance.

I have a client whose mother lived out of town in a small home she owned. She had no real savings, just enough money to cover a couple of months of living expenses and social security. When her health started to fail, my client told his mother (he was single) that he would buy a bigger home and move her in and take care of her for as long as he could. His mother agreed, but only on the condition that he would allow her to take the proceeds from the sale of her home to help pay her share of utilities.

He knew this would let his mother feel she was paying her own way and keep her pride intact. She agreed to the plan and he bought a larger home on one floor. He took care of his mother for several years until she could not stay at home any longer. She had developed Alzheimer's disease and, for her safety, she was moved to a nursing home.

She had enough home sale proceeds left to pay for several months of care. When her cash was gone and all she had was her Social Security, her son applied for Medicaid. She qualified and Medicaid paid her bill for several months. Several months after her death my client received a letter from a local law firm hired by the state for Medicaid recovery. The law firm informed him it was going to recover the $60,000 Medicaid had spent on her care. Medicaid was convinced my client's mother had been paying the mortgage and they wanted $60,000 from him or the agency would put a lien on his home.

It was an incredibly intimidating letter that made him sick to his stomach. He was a professional, had a good job, and had made every house payment. His mother had given him half the utility expenses every month, just as they had agreed. Long story short, he had many weeks of sleepless nights, worrying about losing his home and the small fortune he was spending on legal bills. In the end, he kept his home, and his lawyers acted as if they had given him a break and let him off easy.

Get Your Ducks in a Row

1. *Medicaid helps people who qualify for assistance pay for long-term care.*

2. *Medicaid restricts asset gifts that are given within 60 months of the start of Medicaid assistance.*

3. *Medicaid will try to "recover" assets from a Medicaid patient's estate at that person's death.*

🦆 | CHAPTER 4

Picking a Long-Term Care Option

So What Does It All Mean?

It means an extended stay can easily cost $6,000 a month for custodial care and $8,000 a month for continuous care. Purchasing long-term care insurance is the easiest fix, but it is also costly. My overwhelming experience is even people who can easily afford long-term-care insurance don't want to spend the money—even though they know one month's bill from a nursing home is more than enough to pay for an entire year's worth of insurance premiums.

You have some real choices in preparing for long-term-care costs, but you have to get started. First, you can bite the bullet and purchase nursing home insurance early enough to make it affordable so the increases in premiums (yes, they are coming) won't force you to abandon your policy later in life. Buying a policy from someone who really understands your personal financial position is very important. If you discover the daily cost of care in your area, for example, is $150 a day, a professional (not just a salesman) will take into account your current income and may determine you only need to purchase, or insure, for maybe $100 a day. If you consider the odds are good that you will qualify for Medicare for the first 20 days, then a first-day coverage policy doesn't make sense, and maybe a 30- or 90-day elimination (self-pay) policy is more appropriate. The duration of your coverage for nursing home care is also important. According to Medicare, approximately 43 percent of people over the age of 65 are likely to spend time in a nursing home. Of these, 24 percent will be there less than one year. According to the National Nursing Home Survey, females spend slightly more time in nursing homes than do males—2.51 years compared to 2.29 years. People over the age of 85 have a longer average length of stay at 2.62 years. So why would you pay for a policy that charges you for a benefit covering five years to a lifetime? Following these simple guidelines will save you up to 40 percent or more of your policy cost!

Your second option is to plan early and do what I like to call controlled gifting. Controlled gifting is a simple concept that a lot of my clients prefer to paying for long-term-care insurance. Imagine three buckets, one for the money you need today to live on, a second bucket for tomorrow's needs, including buying a new car every three to five years, installing a new roof, appliances, and so on, and a third bucket for, hopefully, *never*. This third bucket can hold money or assets that you really believe you will never have to use. Instead of just giving the assets to your kids to lose in a divorce, lawsuit or their own health care disaster, and to get these assets out of your estate, you can gift them to a trust for the benefit of your kids and grandkids at your death. You can name your most trusted child as trustee. After the 60-month Medicaid look-back period, you're home free and the assets are safe—see Figure 1.

Everyone has three buckets of money!

Today   Tomorrow   Never

Fig. 1

Money to Live on for Three to Five Years Needs Money to Protect

Your third option is to purchase life insurance (yes, life insurance) and let a life insurance trust own the policy. A life insurance trust is a trust that can own your insurance policy instead of you owning it. After a look-back period, the insurance value does not count as an asset against you. The trust will allow someone you trust, usually one of your kids, to be the trustee and control the policy. The life insurance premium gifted to the trust would be similar to long-term-care insurance premiums, but you would be purchasing tax-free life insurance that would replace your cash spent on nursing home care or health care later in life. It is a simple concept that works. A client of mine who recently went into a nursing home has funded a life insurance policy in an insurance trust for the past several years that has a $350,000 face value. His family is using his taxable IRA RMD (required minimum distribution) to pay his monthly medical bills and will take a health care medical deduction against the income tax liability on his income tax return. He is trading a part of the taxable IRA account for tax-free life insurance left to his family and protected in a trust. Knowing the average stay in a nursing home and his situation, he will not spend anywhere near the face amount of the life insurance. If he had not gone into a nursing home, the entire insurance value would have passed to his kids. Many of the newest life insurance policies have a long-term-care rider that will allow a family to pay their relative's nursing home bills by writing a check each month against the face amount of the insurance death benefit. What has not been used at death is paid to the beneficiary as a tax-free death benefit.

Your fourth option is a new long-term-care rider that can be added to a life insurance policy. The rider option actually allows you to access a part of your death benefit face amount while you are still alive to help pay your long-term-care bills. Because this is a rider option, it is more costly than regular life insurance, but for some folks, it is a great option and cheaper than long-term-care insurance.

Your fifth option is to not have a plan and pay the bill dollar for dollar—not a great option.

Get Your Ducks in a Row

1. *Determine if your current income will cover the cost of a nursing home stay.*

2. *If your income is not sufficient, determine how much savings you are willing to spend on long-term care.*

3. *Choose an option early to create a plan that best suits your financial position and review it on an annual basis.*

🦆 | CHAPTER 5

Social Security Wise

Making an uninformed decision on when to take Social Security could really cost you *big* money over the years. Most folks are aware that the age at which you begin receiving Social Security benefits impacts the amount of your monthly benefits. If you start collecting before your full retirement age—currently age 66—your benefit will be reduced. If you wait until age 70, the amount will be higher by at least 32 percent (your benefit is increased by 8 percent for every year you delay taking your benefits). That could amount to the interest earned every year on a $100,000 investment, without having the investment!

> *Every year you wait to file for benefits increases your benefit by 8 percent!*

Few people are aware that if you are married, waiting at least until full retirement age to start taking Social Security benefits gives you additional options in terms of how you take your benefits, and the impact on both you and your spouse can really be significant.

File and Suspend

When you have reached full retirement age, "file and suspend" is most useful when one spouse is older than the other is. Here is how it works:

Let's say Greg is 66 and Amy is 62. If he filed to start receiving benefits today, Greg would receive $2,000 a month. However, delaying the start of his Social Security payments until he is 70 would increase his monthly benefit by at least 32 percent (4 x 8 percent). Greg will also get the annual cost-of-living adjustments that Social Security recipients get during those years.

Amy, however, wants to start receiving Social Security benefits now. She would get $700 a month if she were of full retirement age. By starting four years early, her benefit would be reduced to $525 a month.

She also can't claim a spousal benefit based upon Greg's earnings; she's not entitled to this until he has filed for Social Security.

What If You Start and I Wait?

Greg can file for benefits and at the same time ask Social Security to suspend them (not send any payments). Since he has, technically, filed, even though he is not getting payments, Amy is now entitled to a spousal benefit. The amount of her check will be the amount she earned on her own work record or her spousal benefit, whichever is higher. Since Amy is under her full retirement age, the amount will be reduced. In this example, Amy's spousal benefit is higher, so she will receive $735 a month.

Three months before turning 70, Greg notifies Social Security that he would like to begin receiving a monthly check. Assuming an annual cost of living adjustment of 3 percent, Greg's monthly check will now be $2,971 a month, nearly 50 percent higher than his age 66 benefit.

"File and suspend" is an option that allows one spouse to greatly increase the size of his or her own benefit, while allowing the other spouse to qualify for spousal benefits.

SOCIAL SECURITY BENEFITS
Full retirement age

Year of Birth	Age
1943-54	66
1955	66 + 2 months
1956	66 + 4 months
1957	66 + 6 months
1958	66 + 8 months
1959	66 + 10 months
1960 & Later	67

Source: ssa.gov

Restrict the Scope

Another strategy that is available once you reach full retirement age is called "file to restrict the scope" of your benefit. It works when both spouses are at least of full retirement age and both have earned a Social Security benefit.

Let us suppose married couple Greg and Amy both turn 66, full retirement age, this year. Amy's benefit will be $2,500 a month and Greg's benefit will be $1,800.

Greg goes ahead, files for Social Security, and receives $1,800 a month based upon his own work record.

Amy files her application but asks Social Security to restrict the scope of her benefit, paying her only what she is entitled to as a spouse. Since Amy is of full retirement age, her spousal benefit is 50 percent of Greg's, or $900 a month.

Four Years Later

Two months before her seventieth birthday, Amy asks Social Security to stop her spousal benefit and begin paying her the benefit she earned, based upon her own work record.

After four years of taking the Delayed Retirement Credit, and assuming annual cost-of-living adjustments of 3 percent, Amy's monthly check will grow to $3,713, almost 50 percent higher than what she would have received four years earlier.

The lesson learned is that if you can afford to postpone Social Security benefits at least until full retirement age, there can be a lot at stake. There are several things to consider, such as your health, family longevity, and cash in retirement plans. A good estate planner can chart your personal Social Security options by using your real numbers to help you decide what is best for you. If you want to learn more, you can go to my Social Security information site at ggentry. sswise.com and request a free report.

🦆 | CHAPTER 6

What Else Might I Need?

There are four documents that I insist you have if I am going to take you on as a client. You have to want to have a plan as badly as I want you to have one, and I want to know without doubt who is in charge of your affairs when you no longer can be.

The first document is a financial power of attorney, which is a legal document an attorney can prepare for you. It states who will have your permission to make financial decisions for you should you not be able to. If you are married, most often, your spouse would serve as your "attorney in fact" and you would name, as a backup, a child who could step up to make sure your finances stay in order, that taxes, utility bills, and insurance bills are paid, that you take your RMD payments, and so on. It is

It makes sense for you to decide now who will handle your affairs in case you become physically or mentally incapacitated rather than leaving the decision to a court.

important to name a backup who could be relied upon, not just a relative who lives closest or a first-born.

The second document is a health care power of attorney, in which you name the person or people who can make health care decisions on your behalf should you not be able to. They can decide what hospital or nursing home you go to, which doctor to see, what medication is right, and so on. Again, if you are married, your spouse usually is your first choice and you can name as many second choices as you want. A lot of times I will tell clients, if they travel on a regular basis to see out-of-town kids or grandkids, they could name all their kids as backups, and whoever was closest in a time of need could handle any issues until everyone in the family could be contacted. Health care power of attorney forms are usually handed out free of charge in senior citizen centers.

Rather than having a separate estate planner, financial planner, insurance agent, attorney and tax preparer, I always recommend you use a "team" approach. Not only will you find it cheaper but everybody's on the same page.

The third document is a living will, in which you give direct instructions to your family and doctor if you are put on life support. Last but not least, is a will or trust to distribute your assets. Not having a will or trust—or "dying intestate"—most often is a costly, slow process that will lead to family conflict. If you do not have a will, the state will create one for you and will decide who gets what.

Get Your Ducks in a Row

1. *People don't plan to fail; they fail to plan. You need these documents* before *you need them.*

2. *Most senior citizen centers offer these documents free of charge or make them available at a reduced cost.*

3. *Make sure the people named in these documents have their own copies.*

🦆 | CHAPTER 7

*Increasing Your Estate Size
While Reducing Taxes!*

The life insurance industry is perhaps the largest crooked industry in the world (or it may be second to the investment industry). But as a result, the life insurance industry has some of the best lobbyists walking the halls in Washington DC and some incredible deals have been struck, in your favor. Life insurance allows you to turn pennies into dollars and if you understand the tax benefits you are allowed to take advantage of, your family can win big! You can set up a life insurance trust to "own" your insurance policy. You pick your beneficiaries and decide how they can take the money out at your death and you pick who will be your trustee to oversee the trust. Let me give you an example of how it can work. I am 53 years old and this year I purchased a million-dollar, term-to-age-100, life-insurance policy that costs me $228 a month, or $2,736 a year.

My insurance trust owns the policy and one of my kids is the trustee. I will gift the premium to the trust each year and there is no tax liability to anyone at the end of the year. I set the trust up to fund an educational fund (as outlined in my trust) for my future grandkids and great grandkids. It's great for my grandkids and their education and it's great for my great-grandkids' kids, because they don't have to pay for their kid's education, which allows them to save more for their retirement. And don't forget it's great for me because I'm buying dollars for pennies. If I live to age 90, I will trade $100,862 in premiums for $1,000,000 of *tax-free* life insurance protection from everything bad!

Let me ask you a stupid question. Do you think income and death taxes are going to continue to go up over the next 37 years or go down? I just avoided them. The best part for me and my wife is we feel we can spend some more of our money in retirement, knowing we planned ahead with tax-free insurance.

> *For a lot of people, it really makes sense to buy dollars with pennies later in life. You're not buying insurance because you "need it"; you're buying it to use as a tool.*

Recently, an 80-year-old female client of mine lost her husband and in reviewing her situation, she decided she had $300,000 to put in her "never" bucket. She had an attorney set up an insurance trust and we funded the trust with the $300,000 of cash. We then purchased a $680,000 life insurance policy (owned by the trust) and the trust will pay $50,000 a year in premiums for five years. She will trade $250,000 of taxable cash for $680,000 of tax-free life insurance, protected in a trust for the benefit of her kids and grandkids. By the way, she still has $50,000, left in cash, added to the $680,000 which totals $730,000. You have to admit that beats the 1.10 percent CD it came out of.

I could give you example after example of similar cases. The hard part is getting over the fact you're buying life insurance. Unfortunately, a large percentage of life insurance agents today sell insurance because they can't find work doing anything that will pay as much as insurance commissions. I have struggled with these "professionals" for almost 35 years because all they want to do is sell you something. They really do not have the knowledge to help you with a real plan. The mistrust the public has of the insurance industry has been well earned.

Try to find a real professional and you will be surprised at what that professional can do for you and your estate. Remember, there is a big difference between buying something and being sold something.

Life insurance has actually gotten cheaper over the last 10 to 15 years and policy design is so much better that converting older policies can really make sense and give you more bang for your buck.

Another tip on saving money through insurance is to insure your adult kids or son-in-law or daughter in-law. What? Okay, let's say your daughter married a less-than-enterprising young man, barely making a living and grandkids come along. The son-in-law gets killed in a car wreck with no savings or insurance. Any guesses as to who now uses their retirement money to raise a second family instead of enjoying retirement? If that son-in-law is 27 years old, you can pay to insure him for $250,000 for 20 years for $180 a year in premiums. Is it worth it?

Get Your Ducks in a Row

1. *Review your current life insurance policies and determine what your real need for life insurance is. Do you need to replace income for a spouse, estate planning, increasing estate size, or tax planning?*

2. *When you determine your real need, get multiple company quotes to see what is available to you today. You will be surprised.*

3. *If your health is better than average, consider life insurance with a long-term-care rider.*

🦆 | CHAPTER 8

Some Good Reasons to Roll Your
401(K) into an IRA

M ost 401(k)s and other company plans have limited investment options. They may offer 50 different mutual funds and other investments options, but most of the options are subject to market fluctuations. If we learned anything in 2008 and early 2009, it's that what the market gives can be taken away with little to no warning. Many of these accounts lost as much as 30 percent in 2008 alone. Those who chose to play it safe and moved their 401(k) money into bond funds or funds invested in CDs and other short-term investments were rewarded with little or no growth while inflation and management fees ate away at their principal. IRAs have almost unlimited investment options including annuities that guarantee the principal and offer a competitive rate of return.

Plan Guidelines Can Restrict the Owner's Access to Money

The plan document is essentially the 401(k) rulebook. If it's not in the book, you can't do it! With savings down and unemployment up, you never know when you may need access to your retirement accounts. IRAs offer greater flexibility, allowing the owners to make their own rules if they are willing to pay the tax on the distributions.

Direct Rollovers Avoid the 20 Percent Mandatory Tax Withholding

It is critical that the funds are moved as a trustee-to-trustee transfer. If a check is written to the 401(k) owner, you can count on the custodian withholding 20 percent for the IRS and getting a letter from the IRS at some point down the road. I have worked with several clients who have encountered this problem, and they are still battling with the IRS to get the 20 percent withholding back where it belongs or trying to convince the IRS they did not take the money and go to Vegas.

I have always been a big fan of the saying: when you leave, your money leaves with you!

The Biggest Tax Benefit?

A great benefit of rolling over your 401(k) balances into your IRA is an estate planning strategy that can be utilized by your beneficiaries. This strategy is known as a "stretch IRA." The IRS allows younger beneficiaries (children, for example) to stretch distributions of their inherited IRA over their life expectancy, possibly resulting in decades of additional tax-deferred growth. The best way to maximize your IRA is to let it grow tax-deferred for as long as possible.

Some 401(K) Plans Do Not Allow the Roth IRA Conversion.

After a Roth conversion tax is paid, the new Roth will grow tax-free and distributions after the five-year holding will also be income-tax-free. This can be a great benefit to some families. The Pension Protection Act simplified Roth conversions from 401(k)s, 403(b)s and other company-sponsored plans. Beginning in 2010, 401(k) and 403(b) owners could convert company-sponsored plans directly to a Roth 401(k) or Roth 403(b) option. However, your plan must allow such a conversion and actually have these options active in the plan. Every 401(k) plan has its own rules and you have to play by its rules.

If you are considering taking early retirement before age 59½, generally, you have to pay a 10 percent early withdrawal penalty. You can avoid this penalty, however, by taking advantage of the substantially equal periodic payments rule 72(t). This rule allows you to avoid the early-withdrawal penalty as long as you agree to withdraw a specific amount of money for five years or until you turn 59½, whichever is longer. You will still owe income taxes on your withdrawals, but avoiding the 10 percent penalty tax is a big deal.

Get Your Ducks in a Row

1. *When you retire and leave, your money leaves with you.*

2. *Consider rolling from a 401(k) or 403(b) into an IRA where you can take control of your retirement funds and plan to stretch the funds.*

3. *Work with an advisor who keeps up with current tax code changes and keeps you informed. It's not just about what you make; it's about what you keep.*

🦆 | CHAPTER 9

To Trust or Not to Trust?

When I started a family, I went to our family attorney and told him I thought I needed a will, and he said, "Absolutely. Smart move. You're thinking ahead." The problem was he wasn't thinking ahead, and I didn't know any better. I owned a business. I was married and having kids. I was never given the option of a living trust, and I'm not convinced my attorney even knew it was an option. I would like to think if I had been given the option between a simple will and a living trust, I would have picked no probate, no delays, privacy and controlled distributions for my children with no court involvement. This was not what I got.

A simple living trust allows you to be your own trustee (the person in charge, or couple if married) and decide exactly who will receive your assets and under the terms you decide. A trust allows your assets to be held for your grandkids' education or whatever is important to you. You can bypass the son or daughter-in-law and make sure your grandkids receive your assets if your kids predecease you. There is no probate or public disclosure.

Fifteen years after the fact, I asked the attorney who wrote my will why I wasn't given the option of a trust and, incredibly, he told me I didn't ask for one. My mistake it turns out was thinking he would tell me what was best for me and my family, especially as he was a family friend. Maybe you have made the same mistake.

My opinion is that most attorneys don't want you to avoid probate because of the money to be made probating your estate. I had an attorney tell me years ago, "You're right. There are a lot of people out there who should have a living trust and I wish I could write them for your clients, but I can't afford to be blackballed by the other attorneys in town." For years, many attorneys have hidden behind the excuse that most people don't have enough money to need a trust, which makes it a net worth issue. The reality, today, is that most clients' biggest fear is having adult children with mixed families from second marriages and making sure the right people get what they are supposed to get. Many people also have family issues and don't want the estate to go through the probate process in which everyone can see what they had and read the will to see who gets what. If you have kids or grandkids who cannot control money, a trust allows you to control distributions. The reasons go on and on and the bottom line is the choice should be yours. Most attorneys have this magical way of talking down to you and making you feel incompetent to the point you just stop asking questions. It is incredibly frustrating.

So let me give you a scenario of what could have happened to me when I had young kids and was driving 40,000 miles a year to start

> *A living trust is not created for asset protection against a disability or spend-down. You have to know what it will and will not do. It is not a fix-all remedy.*

a business. If I had been killed in a car accident and gone through probate and my family wanted to sell my business, the value of my business share, including cash and tangible assets, value of inventory, life insurance, investments, buy-sell agreements—everything—would have been on public record in probate court. If someone had the ability to look into my finances, do you think a prospective buyer of my business would have given me an honest bid, or one based on what my finances told them my family had to have to sell the business?

The scary thing for a business owner is that in many courthouses, because of the Freedom of Information Act, for $1 a page, you can walk out with a copy of anything you want from the probate file, including a copy of the will. Where do you think brokers get some of their best leads? They get the heirs' names, addresses and how much they will be receiving and start sending them investment newsletters long before they even have the money to invest. The beneficiaries think it's fate; I call it a setup.

As good as it sounds, a living trust is not for everyone. It depends on your estate complexity, size and family dynamics. However, as I said, the decision should be yours on whether to go through probate or not, letting your affairs be private or public, deciding who will control your estate at death or while you're living if incapacitated, who gets your assets if your married daughter dies—the son-in-law or your grandkids—how fast or slow the estate can be distributed.

Who Really Owns What?

It is very common to see the name of a trusted adult child on bank accounts, investment accounts and sometimes even on the title to real estate or a home. The reason people do this is that if they become disabled, this child will be able to pay their bills and take care of their personal business. In the event of their death, this child can be relied on to distribute cash and other assets to the other siblings. This plan often leads to unpleasant results and can tear a family apart.

How you own an asset takes precedent over how a will or trust can actually distribute the asset. Let me give you an example. A few years ago, a lady came to my office with her four children. The lady owned a very valuable piece of real estate worth over a million dollars and a CD worth $100,000. The real estate was the small family farm she had grown up on. Over the years, the town she lived in grew around the property. The buildings had long since been torn down, but the family kept the property mowed and looking nice. Here is the rest of the story. Mother was 101 years old and the kids ranged from 75 to 83. She had gone to an attorney a few months before and told the attorney she wanted her assets to pass to her kids without being tied up in probate. The attorney put the farm and the CD in her and her oldest son's name as joint tenants with rights of survivorship, so it would avoid probate just as she had requested. (Watch what you ask for!) A new will was prepared, naming the oldest son as executor and giving all the kids an equal share of the estate. The problem was when mother died, the oldest son owned the farm and CD outright. Survivorship means the last person alive owns the asset, so there is nothing in the will to pass on. The assets belonged to the oldest son and the other kids were cut out of Mom's estate. All the kids immediately looked at the older son and before they could say anything, he told them, "You know I will give you your share." I think he really would have, but my question for the siblings was what if the older son died or became sick before the gift was made? Would his wife or kids still make the gift? What about a nursing home look-back period? If he went into a nursing home within five years, would they have to give everything back?

When someone adds the name of someone else to the title of his or her property, creating joint property ownership, that person also receives the tax basis (original cost) of that property. When the surviving joint owner sells the property, the tax treatment would be the same as if the original owner had sold the property. The estate would lose its "step-up" in basis and be liable for the capital gains tax. This can be a very costly mistake, a lot more than probate would have cost. The estate tax law allows a significant exemption in calculating capital gains on appreciated property, which is part of an estate. When people pass away, their heirs receive a "step-up" in their basis. The tax basis for the heirs is the value of the property on the date of death, not on the date the property was acquired, usually, with the result that no gains tax is due!

Types of Joint Property Ownership

First, you need to understand the various types of joint ownership. There are three categories of joint ownership:

- joint tenants with rights of survivorship

- tenants in common

- tenants by the entireties

If you wish to use joint ownership to pass property, following the death of a spouse, usually, you create a joint tenancy with rights of survivorship (JTROS or JTWROS) account. At the death of one of the joint tenants (spouse), the property automatically becomes the property of the surviving joint owner. Instead of you each owning 50 percent, you each own 100 percent. When two or more people own property as tenants in common, the property does not automatically go to the surviving joint tenants on death. Rather, the decedent's interest in the property goes to his or her estate. This means spouses might have to probate a share to the surviving spouse.

Different banks and financial firms can have their own interpretation of how the different types of account ownerships work. If you use more than one bank or firm, do not assume all the accounts will work the same. You must ask. Survivorship, tenants in the entirety, tenants in common, and/or POD, TOD. They all do something different. Do you know which one you have?

Trusts and Gifting.

You can use an irrevocable or hybrid insurance trust to provide protection for your assets from future long-term-care costs, taxes, grandkids' college funds or potential family problems. A well-drafted irrevocable trust will allow you to gift assets to family members without exposing the money to their creditors or creating potentially large, capital gains taxes. You can be the grantor (the person giving). One of your kids can be the trustee (the person who controls the trust assets), and your kids, grandkids or anyone else can be beneficiaries.

The gift tax is incredibly misunderstood by most people. There are two levels of exemption from the gift tax. First of all, gifts of up to the annual exclusion ($14,000 per recipient, as of 2013) are not subject to tax or income tax filing requirements. Tuition or medical expenses you pay for someone (the educational and medical exclusion) don't count against your $14,000 exemption. Married couples can each give this amount tax-free to the receiver. A gift giver can give to any number of recipients and the exclusion is not affected by other gifts that recipient may have received from others.

Second, if you give above the current gifting limit ($14,000 per recipient), you file a gift tax form with your income taxes and the overage is deducted from your current lifetime estate basic exclusion amount, which was $5,250,000 in 2013. The tax is paid by the gift giver, not the person who receives the gift and only if the gift exceeds the basic lifetime exemption.

> *If a gift tax is due, it is paid by the giver, not the receiver.*

What Is an IRA Trust and Why Might I Want One?

An IRS ruling recently approved a specially designed IRA trust that offers protection and flexibility while allowing the beneficiaries to "stretch" their shares of the IRA over their life expectancies. Having spent a great deal of time studying the IRA distribution rules and the advantages of using an IRA trust, I am now recommending them to just about every client whose retirement account balance exceeds $200,000. Individual retirement accounts (IRAs) were not originally designed to be wealth transfer vehicles. However, effective January 1, 2003, the IRS issued new regulations with respect to Internal Revenue Code 401(a) (9), the code section that outlines rules that allow IRAs to be stretched out to family members.

The key aspect of these regulations is that they now permit a nonspouse beneficiary to "stretch" the taxable required minimum distributions over his or her (actuarial) lifetime. The ability to compound the IRA investments, tax-free, over a much longer period of time makes IRAs now one of the most valuable tools when passing wealth down from generation to generation.

Think about It

A $200,000 IRA, inherited by a 50-year-old, could be worth $1.5 million or more over his and his children's lifetimes! In other words, obtaining the maximum income tax stretch should be a prime planning objective. This income tax stretch can be obtained either by naming individuals as beneficiaries or by naming a trust as a beneficiary.

However, naming individuals as beneficiaries may create a host of other problems:

- The individual beneficiary may at any time decide to take out more than the required minimum distributions (RMDs) because he is not aware of the tax rules and the choices he has, or he gets bad advice, or he (or his spouse) simply wants to spend the money, and he thereby causes the taxation to occur much earlier, loses years of tax-free compounding, and essentially wastes the stretch.

- The original account owner does not control who will eventually inherit the IRA assets after the primary beneficiary.

- The beneficiary may have poor money management skills, be a spendthrift or too young or disabled to manage money.

- The IRA is exposed to the beneficiary's spouse in a divorce.

- A beneficiary receiving government benefits could lose them.

- Lawsuits against the beneficiary and his creditors could take the IRA.

Even if none of the above occurs, what could represent a substantial sum when the beneficiary dies may then be subject to estate taxes when it goes down to the next generation.

All of these problems may be dealt with by naming a trust as a beneficiary. Unfortunately, under the IRS regulations, a trust named as a beneficiary must jump through a number of hoops in order for the RMDs to obtain maximum stretch-out over the lifetime of the beneficiaries of the trust. A living trust, typically, cannot meet all of these requirements and, therefore, a separate trust, called the IRA trust, can be set up as the IRA beneficiary.

The IRA trust is specially designed to not only meet the IRS requirements for a "designated beneficiary trust" in order to obtain maximum income tax stretch-out, but it also provides protection against all of the above problems that may occur when an individual is named beneficiary. Amazingly, this trust is revocable by the grantor (owner) and beneficiaries to give them protection against possible future tax changes.

I am just saying that, more often than not, you get what you pay for.

It certainly seems as if there is a trust for everything. Let me give you some warning in advance. In my 32 years of experience in financial and advanced estate planning I have come to realize that unless attorneys are in a large firm where they can specialize in one area—as a doctor does—or have a single attorney practice focusing just on estate planning or probate, they have to become a jack of all trades. There is a divorce hearing at 9 a.m., a dog bite case at 11 a.m., a house closing at 2 p.m., a car crash at 3 p.m. and a property fence dispute at 4:30 p.m.

I am not saying all single attorney firms are bad, because I know some great ones. I am just saying that, more often than not, when it comes to trusts or advanced estate plans, you get what you pay for. It is extremely important to have a property trust drafted by a competent, trust-experienced attorney.

When I realized my clients had to have the option of a living trust, after a long and exhausting search, I found a great estate-planning attorney. This gentleman, who was also a CPA, had an office about an hour away and worked with many professional athletes in Ohio. I created a great information folder that contained a wealth of estate planning information so I would have something that clients could easily read to see what their options were. I did workshops on a regular basis, and after one workshop, a man came up to me to book an appointment for the next afternoon. An engineer in his late forties, he worked at a local factory and looked after his mother. She was not in great health and had a large estate, so he was interested in ways to protect her estate and avoid probate. We met for over two hours and I answered hundreds of questions and outlined all the options she had. He had my folder and I loaned him books, magazines and reports and encouraged him to call the attorney we teamed with. He thanked me for all the information and said he would call back in a couple of days and set a follow-up appointment. He never called back. All the contact information he gave me was fake, and I lost all the information I had loaned him.

Several months later, I was asked to speak on retirement planning at a local financial fair that a women's group was hosting. It was an all-day affair and I was booked to do three sessions. After my first workshop, I had a session off, so I looked at the agenda and saw that an attorney was conducting a living trust workshop. I was excited because I thought this might be another attorney option for my clients and decided to go to his session and sit in the back and talk to him when he was finished. I walked into the session, sat down in the back, and picked up a workshop folder on the chair. To my amazement, the folder was full of nothing but the information that I had spent hours putting together. Someone else's logo had been put on it. I looked up and the attorney walked to the front of the room and introduced himself as the area's leading trust and estate planning expert. I had never heard of him. Of course, you know the rest of the story. It was the "engineer" who had lied about everything and taken all my information. About 10 minutes into the workshop, he saw me and turned as red as a fire truck, and he never recovered. At the end of the workshop, people started to put their hands up and ask him questions. He fumbled through. When everyone was finished, I stood up in the back and asked him how people could find a good, ethical attorney, because I did not know any. He never said a word and walked out of the room. I never asked for my information back because I thought the sight of it would make him look over his shoulder and maybe force him to clean up his act. To this day, 25 years later, he still advertises himself as the trust expert.

Get Your Ducks in a Row

1. *There is trust for everything. Know what you're trying to accomplish and find a quality trust attorney so you're not sold something you don't need.*

2. *Ownership takes precedent over a will or trust, so know how your assets are titled.*

3. *Don't try to please everyone. Take the time to pick the right person to be in charge of your estate.*

🦆 | CHAPTER 10

Here I Come to Save the Day!

Remember the old Mighty Mouse cartoon and the theme song, "Here I Come to Save the Day?" It's funny to look back on it now, but it's not so funny when somebody in your family plays it today at your expense. This is a frustrating topic to deal with, but one I see people have to deal with every day.

Here is the scenario: Dad has passed away. Mom cannot stay by herself 24 hours a day but does not need to be in a nursing home. You have a sister and a brother (insert your siblings here). You live close to Mom. Your sister lives three hours away and your brother lives out of state.

You are the one who ran your father to the doctor and your mom to the store and checked on them every day the whole time your dad was sick before he passed. Not your sister or brother. Now mom needs to live with someone, only she doesn't want to leave her friends or church. Any guess what happens next? Yep, you move Mom in with you, but you also packed up all those years of memories from

> *The key is to start the discussion of this topic long before the time for action comes.*

her home and unpacked them at yours. You might have even been in charge of selling Mom's home (after you cleaned it, cared for it and made sure the grass was cut by you or your husband). Your single sister can't really help because she has a small house, doesn't feel well, has to help with her grandkids, is always on vacation, is busy at church, has a backache, doesn't like to drive, and so on, and so on. Your brother would like to help but lives out of state. He really supports you when he doesn't have to take sides with you or your sister. Here is the kicker ("Here I come to Save the Day!"): every time your sister comes to town, she feels the need to tell you, and all her friends, everything she thinks you have been doing wrong. Obviously, she is trying to somehow make herself look better by making you look bad. Unfortunately, sometimes it works with people who do not know the rest of the story and that adds to the frustration.

In addition, your sister wants to make sure you are not squandering her inheritance (Mom's money) on anything foolish such as Mom's living expenses while Mom is living, free of expenses, in your home where, for the most part, your life has ended as you knew it.

It will drive you completely insane. Any of this sound familiar? I hope not, but I know too many people in this situation right now who knew it was coming but did not know how to prepare for it.

The key is to start the discussion of this topic long before the time for action comes. If you are the responsible child, you know you are the one who is going to end up taking care of Mom. You love Mom, but you know what it is going to do to your life. You need to discuss with your single sister the option of her moving in with Mom before Mom needs the help. You must explain to your sister that her living expenses would go down because Mom would still be paying the monthly bills. You should share the conversation with your brother and ask him how he would feel about taking Mom for the summer or winter. After your siblings balk or give you reasons why they couldn't possibly help out, you have a narrow window open to tell them your rules on how things are going to work. This is only a narrow window, so you have to make it count. Take nothing for granted and set the rules early. First, you are the only acting power of attorney for your mom. Your siblings should serve as backups if you cannot serve, but you are the boss. You are the only health care power of attorney and your siblings should be backups. Just stop and imagine the frustration of being the responsible child who is doing everything, yet constantly being told how she should be doing things differently.

If mom has funds or even just Social Security, figure what Mom's share of food, utilities, and so on, are on a monthly basis and let everyone know what Mom's share of living expenses would be and put it in writing. Of course, let everyone know the expense will be far less than the $6,000–$8,000 a month assisted living or nursing home expenses would be. Trust me, your mom will understand you need to be reimbursed, and you should. Why would you pay all your mom's bills with your retirement nest egg only to have a nursing home take all the money you saved your mom?

Medicaid does not expect you to spend your savings on your mom's care, but if the agency spends money on your mom, at her death, it will always look to see if there is anything to recapture from her estate.

This is always a hard subject to deal with, but I'm telling you it doesn't make any difference how much you love Mom, at some point in time, the years will become dog years. Not because of Mom, but because of all the other issues you have to deal with in keeping Mom. It doesn't mean you're a bad person or you don't love your Mom. It happens when you realize your own freedom has slipped away because you were the responsible child. By the way, if you are the responsible child, God bless you. You are the real Mighty Mouse.

The most amazing Mighty Mouse story I have been a part of had a surprising hero. A few years ago, my clients included an older, successful, married couple, who had worked hard all their lives, running their own business. The husband died suddenly, and shortly after, the wife's health took a turn for the worse. They had four kids. Two had helped run the business and took over at Dad's death. The other two kids were busy professionals. All the kids were successful, busy, and making money.

Mom's health continued to decline to the point she could not be at home alone. Mom was too ill for assisted living but not ill enough to go into a nursing home. Mom, like most people, did not want someone she didn't know in her home, so the kids decided to take turns taking care of her. That lasted for about three months, but after an emergency family meeting, the kids decided the only answer was for Mom to go to a nursing home. Mom was devastated.

One of the kids had a daughter in her last year of dentistry school. Mom had been helping this granddaughter financially and had given financial help to several of her grandkids. The granddaughter loved her grandmother and had been closely following everything that had been going on. To everyone's surprise, the weekend after the decision had been made to put Mom (Grandmother) in the nursing home, the granddaughter came home and announced she had left school and was moving in with her grandmother to take care of her. The granddaughter told everyone school would always be there, but she only had one grandmother. The granddaughter took care of her grandmother when Grandmother's own kids would not. Grandmother lived a little more than a year and passed away after a short hospital stay, but she never went into a nursing home. To everyone's surprise, during that last year, Grandmother changed her trust and left everything to the granddaughter. Sometimes the real Mighty Mouse can surprise you. By the way, the granddaughter is now a dentist.

Get Your Ducks in a Row

1. *As your parents get older and start to develop minor health issues, engage your siblings in conversations regarding the future care of your parents.*

2. *When a plan starts to develop, share your ideas with your parents and openly discuss what the future plans might be.*

3. *The sibling taking the most responsibility for the care of the parents should have the health care power of attorney.*

🦆 | CHAPTER 11

Bad Advice, Anyone?

When I started in the financial industry over 30 years ago, it did not take me long to figure out that a very large percentage of the people in the industry couldn't care less about their clients. It was all about greed. I have told my clients for years that everyone in the financial industry is a salesperson. We make a living selling things, and not every customer is sold the right thing. Sometimes a salesperson means well but just does not have the knowledge to give the correct advice, so sells the wrong thing. Sometimes the customer is sold the wrong thing out of greed.

I understand why insurance agents remain captive agents (they only write policies for one company) after they have been in the business for a couple of years and start to understand how things work. Let me use life insurance companies as an example. Most life insurance companies have a certain age group of clients they really want to be competitive with. Maybe their clients are 30–40 or 40–50 years old. Some companies prefer older clients aged 65–75. The president of a large life insurance company once told me he wanted to insure every 62- to 69-year-old male he could because that was his best "profit zone" and he couldn't care less about other ages. For years, his company's life insurance premiums were unbeatable for those ages. When I run insurance quotes for estate planning clients, I run a comparison of no less than 12 companies because some companies have small, four- to five-year, buy-in "sweet spots" that make them almost unbeatable in price. How can a captive agent, who only has one company to write business for, expect clients to believe he has the best product 100 percent of the time? Do you know any one product in a competitive market that is the best 100 percent of the time?

A broker in my area spends a tremendous amount of money on advertising in an effort to present himself as a real expert. He is in his fifties and dresses as you would expect a successful advisor to dress and drives what you would expect a successful advisor to drive. He really plays the part. The truth is that until two years ago this expert had sold shoes in a big-box shoe store for 20 years. There is certainly nothing wrong with selling shoes, but when you try so hard to sell yourself as a seasoned advisor with real experience, I have to wonder about the quality of the advice being sold.

Early this year, during a new client discovery interview, I learned that the client's broker at a big-name brokerage firm had moved $600,000 of the client's money into a new, high-risk account without the client's knowledge. The broker had changed brokerage firms and hadn't told the client he had switched companies. The client had no idea the broker was no longer representing the company he thought he was. The broker made a new commission and put the client's money at risk during the process. In reviewing the broker's regulatory history online, we found he had a history of doing this and regulatory fines had been paid in the past, but that hadn't stopped the big names from continuing to hire him because he was a good salesman!

I started on the insurance side of financial services and only sold term insurance and mutual funds to young families. I could sell $250,000 of 20-year, guaranteed, renewable, level term insurance to a young father with kids for $25 a month. Everyone else in the industry was selling $50,000 whole life policies for $50 a month. When I replaced my first whole life policy that an agent from another company had written on a young father, the agent came to my office and called me a crook for replacing his business and he tried to pick a fight. The agent never for one minute considered the benefit to the client and his family. Later, I actually got threatening calls from the agent on my home answering machine, warning me to never do it again. Most clients would be surprised to know how common this behavior is. I am guessing I replaced another 20–25 of his policies over the next year.

Two years later, that first young father whose policy I replaced was killed in a car accident and I gave his widow and two kids a check for $250,000, my first death claim. Shortly after I had delivered the death claim check, I got a call from their former agent's sales manager, who wanted to meet me. Out of curiosity, I agreed and we had lunch. The manager offered me a job selling whole life insurance with his company. There is an old saying in the insurance business, "If you sell term, you can't eat; if you sell whole life, you can't sleep." Needless to say, I kept selling term life insurance.

In the last 30 years, I have only met a small handful of life insurance salesmen and financial advisors who, if asked, were not "expert estate and tax planners," regardless of their experience or education. I think it would surprise you to know how likely it is to get just as much good financial advice at a cocktail party or around the water cooler. Interview your financial people. Don't be fooled by a big company name. Many advisors work with smaller companies because they do not want to get an e-mail from the home office every Monday telling them what to sell clients that week because there is a commission incentive or a trip to win.

> *The distribution phase of retirement, the time when you have to withdraw funds from savings, makes the accumulation part look like child's play.*

Is Your Current Advisor Still Right for You?

Think about it, for the past 30 years, hopefully, your financial planner has been doing primarily one thing: helping you build a nest egg. That's good. You've needed that help. The problem is that the distribution phase of retirement, the time when you have to withdraw funds from savings, makes the accumulation part look like child's play.

When you are working, your paycheck allows you to ride out periodic declines in your investments. However, once you retire, you cannot afford a portfolio—or an advisor—that requires you to sit patiently through bear markets. If you do not want to run out of money before you run out of life. The need for preservation takes the place of the need for accumulation. If you have not saved enough money for retirement, high-risk investments aren't the answer. You shouldn't be retired.

Is your current (accumulation) advisor capable of walking you through the major retirement (distribution) issues such as Medicare and Medicaid planning, nursing home protection, family distributions, avoiding probate issues and income tax strategies? **The fact is, probably not.**

Get Your Ducks in a Row

1. *Keep in mind that all financial advisors are salespeople regardless of how they are paid.*

2. *Make sure your advisor does not offer a one-size-fits-all product from one company. You have to make companies compete for your business.*

3. *Accumulation, distribution and preservation are the three main phases of money management. Be sure you're working with the right person at the right time.*

🦆 | CHAPTER 12

Reverse Mortgage or Not?

irst, let me say that a reverse mortgage is a very different kind of estate planning tool that's not for everyone. But over the last few years many people have told me that a reverse mortgage allowed them to change their lives. A reverse mortgage is a special and very different kind of loan that is easy to obtain if you are at least 62 years old, own your own home or condo with equity, and are willing to go through a few steps to make sure you understand how it works. No credit or financial underwriting is involved; you just have to own a home with equity. These loans are nonrecourse loans, so your house serves as the collateral. A reverse mortgage allows you to convert the equity of your home back into cash for your own use. There is no monthly payment required on the loan, which is, typically, paid back

at the death of the client from the proceeds of the sale of the home by family or the home sale and loan can be a wash. So the million-dollar question is why would someone want to do this?

If you have not been able to save much money for retirement, for whatever reason, but always made your house payment, you probably have found you are asset rich and cash poor, like many people today. So, taking money back out of your house could allow you to do some of the following things people have told me they have been able to do:

A reverse mortgage allows you to convert the equity of your home back into cash for your own use.

• You could hire someone to come to stay in your home part-time to provide health care so you don't have to go to a nursing home before you really need to and end up selling the home to give the cash to Medicaid anyway.

• You could have money to visit your grandkids on a regular basis, and go on a great family vacation every year and pick up the entire bill. You could enjoy your grandkids now while you are able.

• You could buy a badly needed new car, whereas, otherwise, there would have been no extra income to make car payments.

• You could make badly needed repairs to the home you took the loan on. A new kitchen, handicap bathrooms, a new furnace, new sidewalks, new carpet, a new roof, and so on. There is a big difference in owning a nice home and being able to afford to keep living in it! You could pay for your grandkids' educations so they do not have to start life in debt.

- You could give your kids or grandkids a down payment on their own new homes.

- If nothing else, you'd have enough money in the bank to pay all the bills at the end of each month and pay off credit cards for the rest of your life.

- My favorite reason for taking a reverse mortgage comes from a client who took a reverse mortgage for $200,000 and bought a $650,000 tax-free life insurance policy owned by a life insurance trust to leave protected funds to his kids and grandkids.

So many people have told me their kids do not want their parents' home when the parents die because they have moved out of town, or out of state, and will never move back, or the kids make more than the parents ever did and don't need their money.

I think you can see that, for some people, a reverse mortgage offers a good opportunity to turn things around.

Reverse mortgages are highly regulated and there are many reputable companies out there that can assess whether a reverse mortgage is right for you. As with everything else, get the facts in writing, look at the numbers yourself, and make an informed decision.

Get Your Ducks in a Row

1. *Reverse mortgages are highly regulated; it is hard to be rushed into a decision.*

🦆 | CHAPTER 13

The Blind Spot

I had a new client discovery appointment (first appointment) with a husband and wife who were both ready and eager to retire within the next few months and wanted someone to tell them if they had forgotten anything. What I found was a common situation. They had checking and savings accounts at three different banks: he had life insurance with one company; she had insurance policies with two others; he had an IRA with one brokerage firm and a nonqualified brokerage account with another; she had an IRA with yet another, and they each had Roth IRAs at different banks. He had a 401(k) through his employment and she had a 403(b) at hers. He had a will with one attorney and she had a will with another attorney—and a partridge in a pear tree. They have been working with 16 different people for years and none of these professionals ever asked about the others. You would be surprised how common this is. None of these professionals were concerned enough about the clients to make sure they were making money, not mistakes. They were all happy with their little piece of the action. After all these years, it had never dawned on the clients that they did not really have a plan, just a bunch of ideas. It was their "blind spot." They knew they had to save for retirement and they did. They knew they needed a will, so they got one. They knew they did not want all their eggs in one basket, so they diversified. The ideas were good, but the execution was poor.

Checking Accounts		Value	Return
bank 1	his	$2,318.00	0%
bank 2	hers	$6,218.00	0%
bank 3	jt	$3,134.00	0%
Savings			
bank 1	jt	$2,890.00	0.10%
bank 2	jt	$3,398.00	0.10%
Roth IRAs			
bank 1	his	$42,800.00	4.10%
bank 2	hers	$58,300.00	0.08%
IRAs			
brokerage	his	$187,239.00	5.10%
brokerage	hers	$117,777.00	7.20%
Retirement			
401(k)	his	$297,283.00	4.30%
403(b)	hers	$162,387.00	5.10%
Brokerage	his	$32,327.00	14.60%

Who is in charge?

The broker who had their funds in solid investments had never asked the right questions to find out they had more money in horrible investments. The same went for the insurance agents who could have combined the policies and saved the clients a small fortune. Some of the checking and savings accounts at one bank paid interest; some at another bank did not. One Roth IRA was paying 4.1 percent while the other was paying .08 percent.

If you're serious about retirement, protecting your assets and making sure the right people get your assets at your death, it's important to have a team with a coach. Every good coach starts with a plan, implements the plan, and makes corrections when needed. The discovery process is where all the rocks are turned over and all the secrets are told. A good coach (planner) has to have all the information to make the plan work. Look for a copy of the discover sheet that I use with new clients in the back of the book. If no one has ever gotten this kind of information from you before, they are working purely on guesswork and that is not a plan.

Get Your Ducks in a Row

1. *You cannot just save money; you have to have a real plan.*

2. *Your plan must be shared with all the main players and everyone has to be on the same page.*

3. *Pick one of the players to be the "coach" to keep everything on track.*

🦆 | CHAPTER 14

Mapping Out Your Retirement Plan

How much do I have to save every month? Should I max out my 401(k) first or use a Roth IRA? Will Social Security be there for me? What pension withdrawal plan is best? These are some of the most common questions I get and, unfortunately, there is no simple answer that works for everyone. However, let's address these questions and see where it takes us.

How Much Money Do I Have to Save?

This question can be turned around as what do you want to do in retirement? If you want to sit on the front porch in a swing and sip sweet iced tea and watch everyone else drive by, it does not take much money to retire in that style. However, if you had something more in mind, you'd better have a plan. A good financial professional can take all your current numbers, such as income, expenses, the amount you have already saved, projected pension income, projected Social Security income, inflation and the lifestyle you hope to have and find that magic number. I use a great retirement analyzer program and, regardless of where you live, I can find an advisor who will run this analyzer tool for you, free of charge. It is the only real way to know if you are on track or need to make some adjustments.

Should I Max Out My 401(K) or Consider a Roth IRA?

It depends, first, on how good or bad your 401(k) really is. Do you know what your real returns are versus what the plan indicates you are making? I have seen 401(k) statements showing 8 to 12 percent returns on charts, but no matter which way you calculate the percentage, you're making only 4 percent. Some people believe everything they are told. If you're going to win the retirement game, that's got to stop. How much are your plan's enrollment fees? Just because your number (hopefully) gets bigger every year, it doesn't mean you're making money. You yourself are contributing money to that plan. I have seen 401(k)s that were so bad that I have told people they needed to come out of them. So, first, determine if you are in a winner or a dud. The biggest blind spot people have with company retirement plans is failing to see that most of the money is pretax. Figure 1 shows you what you think you have, and Figure 2 shows you what you really have.

Figure 1

Figure 2. Taxes, anyone?

If you understand inflation, you understand you will lose even more of the amount shown in Figure 2. Another blind spot is failing to see you'll retire with every penny of your money in pretax accounts. Therefore, your monthly income is taxable. When you take money out to go to the beach on vacation, it's taxable. When you take money out to buy a new car, it's taxable. When you take money out for Christmas, it's taxable. When your kids need a loan, it's taxable. Get the point? A Roth IRA on the side can give you a break from taxes and help prevent all your withdrawals from becoming a taxable event.

Will Social Security Be There for Me?

I personally believe that if you are in the work force today and pay Social Security taxes, you will probably have Social Security benefits at retirement. I think it may take a different shape in the future, but the government will have to give you some form of value for the money you have already paid in.

What Is the Best Distribution Option for My Pension?

Let me explain an option you might not know anything about called pension maximization. Amy is a teacher getting ready to retire. She has the option of taking a life-only option that will pay her $2,800 a month but leaves her *husband* nothing if she dies before him. A joint-and-100-percent spouse benefit would give Amy a $2,200 a month income while she is alive, and $2,200 a month to her husband, Greg, if she predeceases him. Payments stop at the second spouse's death and nothing passes to kids or grandkids. Nothing. If Amy were eligible for life insurance, she could take the life-only option, live on

$2,300 a month, and purchase a $700,000 life insurance policy with the remaining $500 a month.

The life insurance policy would be purchased inside a life insurance trust and be set up to pay Greg whatever he needed at Amy's death. At Greg's death, the remaining value of the trust passes to the kids and grandkids, protected in a trust. This was the case for one of my clients and it makes a lot of sense to me. The remaining cash was to be left in the trust to be used as an educational trust fund for the kids and grandkids. Very few people even know they have this option, because they are working with the wrong professional. The key factors that might make it work for you are:

> *Remember, every financial person is a salesperson.*

- having at least average health for your age;

- applying for the insurance before the deadline to make sure you're approved for coverage;

- finding the right insurance policy that gives you the biggest "bang" for your buck and has low cash value, if any, and a large face amount;

- making sure your plan allows a surviving spouse not receiving retirement to stay on your health insurance at your death, which is the norm;

- working with a professional who is smart enough to know this is an option and can find the answer for you.

If you are not insurable, have your advisor go over the numbers to determine the best income option for you. Remember, every financial person is salesperson. If it looks to good to be true, get a second opinion. The decision you make is the one you have to live with forever.

Model? What Model?

Today most people who have accumulated a large amount of money in their 401(k) or other investments are able to take advantage of the greatest bull market we have ever seen, from 1982 to the end of 2000. The problem is many people today still have the mindset of that time, and that can be very dangerous. The sooner you realize this is not the same investment world it was even 10 years ago, the better off you will be.

Do you really think you should be investing the same way you did in 2002: ride it out; hang tough; the market always comes back; just hang in there; the market will rebound; just give it time?

These can be dangerous strategies when you are close to retirement or are retired already. During your lifetime, in the big picture, you go through two very distinct money strategy periods: accumulation and distribution. In the accumulation phase, you have time on your side and you can give your accounts the time they need to grow and correct. In the distribution phase, time can be your enemy and many people find themselves running out of money before they run out of life because of poor planning. If you do not stay focused on which phase you are in, it is easy to be tempted out of your phase.

Three Mind Sets of Financial People

My experience is that financial people have three basic mindsets: old school, new school, and no school.

- Old school remembers how it used to be when everything happened for a reason. Times have changed; they haven't.

- New school is like the new doctor in town, full of new ideas and constantly learning.

- No school is the person who is just in it for the money, always puts the client second, and does not intend to stay up to date with anything.

I tell folks who come into my office to look for a person who is not an old-school, know-it-all financial advisor still planning the same way he or she did 20 years ago. There was a time when financial advisors positioned themselves as the person with the expertise in financial planning, investing, different types of insurance, plus basic knowledge about tax, and legal issues such as estate planning. Today one person cannot do it all and the best financial advisors have a team of experts. Financial advisors and estate planners put the plan together. Financial advisors handle the investments. Insurance non-captive experts provide the insurance advice. Qualified tax experts give the tax advice and attorneys handle the legal advice. The advisor or planner is the coach and makes the calls to make sure the client has the right plan. Most people are already paying for all these services, but the right hand doesn't know what the left hand is doing. Remember, the best financial advisors today have a team of experts to help their clients achieve their goals.

With all the financial shows on TV and radio today, hosted by the best "experts" in the industry, it is amazing how you can listen to three shows in a row and get three completely different opinions on what's best for you.

Does History Have a Way of Repeating Itself?

In January 2000 the Dow was almost at 12,000, but it dropped in 2002 to just above 8,000 and in 2007 was back over 14,000. Everyone remembers 2009, when the Dow was just over 6,000 and in late 2013, after many scary up and downs, it was over 16,000. How are you suppose to buy and hold when you are in your retirement years and when was the last time your financial person told you to be safe and sit on the side? From 1896 to 1906, the market had almost a 150 percent cumulative return, but from 1906 to 1924, the cumulative return was more than a 4 percent loss.

From 1929 to 1954 you would have gained a whopping 1.7 percent return. According to a DALBAR analysis, over the last 20 years ending December 31, 2011, the average investor earned 2.1 percent. After inflation, the average investor earned a disheartening -0.4 percent. From January 2000 to the spring of 2012 the Dow grew an average of 0.84 percent per year.

My question to you is what are you or your broker doing so differently from everyone else to not be that average investor? I don't think it is possible when all you have is an annual review or a phone call.

Taking Some Risk off the Table

As you get closer to retirement, you have to start taking some of the risk off the table. When you are young, you can take more risks with your retirement investments because you have a longer time horizon if the market fumbles. As you get closer to retirement, you are moving from accumulation to distribution and it can be a risky move to take "income" from accounts that were set up to give "growth." This doesn't mean just switching to risk investments that are supposed to be more conservative; it means actually eliminating some risk. It is amazing how many nonclients who called my office during the 2008 correction had turned in retirement paperwork and were just days from walking out, only to lose up to 30 percent of their retirement savings. Many canceled their plan to retire.

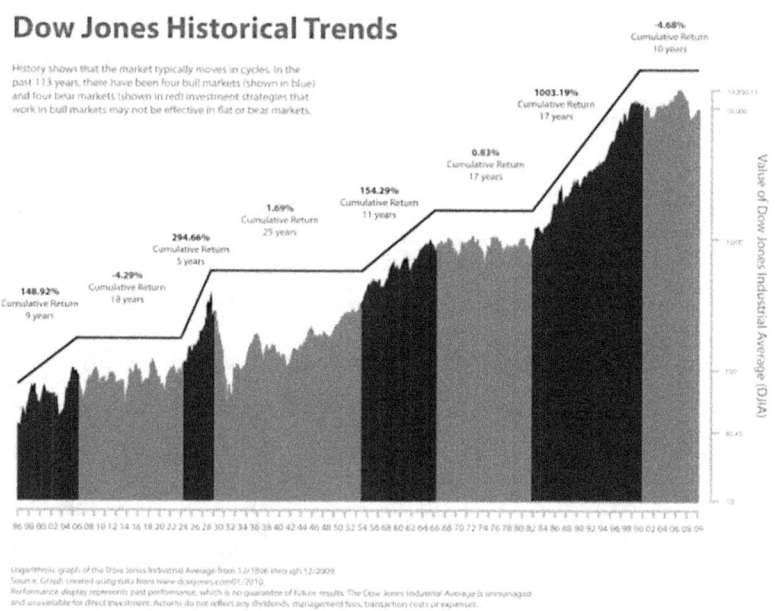

Many financial professionals who understand the need to eliminate some risk at retirement do so by explaining the *three financial worlds*. The first financial stage, or world, for many people is usually a bank.

Maybe your elementary school had a banking day when you learned about money. Maybe, like me, you had a lawn mowing business and, for whatever reason, you knew you had to have some place safe to keep your money. You opened a savings or checking account and your financial experience started. As you got older and started working in a real job, you learned about retirement accounts. You might have had a 401(k), a 403(b), or a similar qualified (IRS approved) account. This is the second stage, or world, of money, where you consult money managers, brokers and financial advisors. Your focus is on growth and your goal is retirement. This is the world where you start to learn about risk as you see your account values go up and down. The third stage, or world, of money is where you find safety and guaranteed income for retirement through insurance companies and annuities. Even though this sounds easy, it is not.

During the '80s and the '90s the market went up and people made money, but over the last decade, the market did not go up. Many call it a long-term flat market and we saw a couple of big drops that were devastating to many people. The markets are so manipulated today that many people feel the market is being controlled like a puppet and can't perform on its own merits. This makes the third world of security and guaranteed income very important. One of my new clients said he was very conservative but had 90 percent of his money in the market because his broker had told him that brokerage firms are a lot smarter today and have better computer models that allow them to put together better strategies and asset diversification. I told my client to ask his broker if he was sure that my client's investments were right for this market, especially knowing he was financially conservative. If my client's accounts lost 20 percent or more before the broker could move the money to safety, would the broker make up the loss out of his own pocket? If not, why was the broker not willing to take that risk personally but was fine with the client taking on that risk?

There are all kinds of formulas to determine how much money you should have in the market. An industry favorite is to deduct your age from 100 and the answer should be the amount you invest in the market. At age 20, then, 80 percent should be in the market. At age 80, 20 percent should be in the market. A broker from a large firm told me his firm uses the age 100 rule but due to current risks, the firm adds an additional 10 percent to the safe money side.

It is simple to me in today's market. I just ask people how much they can comfortably afford to lose. It really makes them stop and think. It is all about risk and reward. How much risk can you afford to take and is the reward worth the risk.

Get Your Ducks in a Row

1. *Every investment prospectus is required to tell you that past performance is no guarantee of future performance, for a reason. Determine your risk tolerance and do not be swayed.*

2. *Sometime market indicators just point in the wrong direction for no reason, especially in today's market. Be open and aware of everything going on around you.*

3. *Be open to change and new products and programs as you look for the "safest, highest return." The financial industry is going through major changes.*

🦆 | CHAPTER 15

Now What?

We have certainly covered a lot of ground and, hopefully, I have given you enough information for you to know if you need more. Before you think about changing anything, I recommend you sit down with an experienced team of professionals to see if any of the ideas discussed in this book will specifically benefit you or your family. No one professional can wear all the hats and be the best at everything. Going out and immediately making changes without all the information you need could actually put you in a worse position. There are some basic rules to follow as you set out to get a plan.

Watch out for information coming from people who do not specialize in the topic you need help with.

If after talking to a planner it still sounds too good to be true, it probably is. Nothing will replace the gut feeling you get. Be smart and trust your feelings.

Watch out for information coming from people who do not specialize in the topic you need help with. If you need heart surgery, you do not go to a foot doctor. Just because he is a doctor does not mean he is the right doctor for you. So, for estate planning, do not go to an attorney who specializes in real estate closings or divorce.

Beware of "online resources" giving specific information. You can Google any financial topic and literally get thousands upon thousands of articles. Half of the articles will be positive and the other half will be negative. Financial salespeople will share articles they think will convince you their pitch is correct, but these articles won't necessarily offer a balanced viewpoint. Do not believe everything you read.

How accomplished are the planners giving you advice? Are they well known? Ask around. Do they have a good name? Do they have professional credentials, and have they been with the same firm for a while? Recently, a new brokerage firm opened an office in a town where my firm does a lot of business. These folks were spending a fortune on advertising telling everyone how good they were. I had never heard of the two top executives, so I ran a broker check on them. I was not so shocked to find that both of them had had serious regulatory issues in the past that had resulted in penalties and financial restitution to clients.

Is your planner listening to you or doing all the talking? If he or she is doing all the talking, you are probably going to be put in a one-size-fits-all situation and just get that famous annual call at the end of the year, which is not a plan. I don't understand how someone can put together a plan for you and your family without listening to what is important to you. An old friend of mine who was in the business longer than I have been used to ask his clients, "Do you want a suit that's on sale, or one that fits?" Take my word on it. Buy the financial suit that fits.

Get Organized

I have included my Discovery Questionnaire in the back of the book, which will help you to gather the information you'll need to start your plan. If you have not been asked all these questions, you do not have a real plan. Take some time to fill the questionnaire out and find a good advisor. If you are not in my practice area and need a trusted advisor, call my office, and wherever you are, I can make a recommendation. Good luck and get your financial ducks in a row!

In Memory of Jim

Early in my career, I met a man who shared many of the same thoughts and concerns that I had about the financial services industry. He was a great sounding board for new ideas and concepts and always told me the truth. For 25 years, I was lucky enough to consider Jim not just a mentor but also a friend, one of those friends you can count on one hand.

He was the best ideas man I have ever known, always looking for a better product, a better program, anything that would put his clients in a better position. He would spend hours figuring out his clients' problems even when he knew there was no financial gain for him. He taught me how important it was to listen to my clients and to build real, personal relationships. He always put his clients first. He always seemed to be on his way to a client's birthday party, a retirement party, a Sunday dinner, a wedding, and even a funeral. Jim was not just an advisor to his clients; he was family. Jim, I thank you for always being on the other end of the phone and teaching me how to do this business the right way—to always buy the suit that fits. You are missed, my friend.

🦆 | MEET THE AUTHOR

Gregory (Greg) Gentry

Greg has over 30 years of experience in the financial and estate planning industry and specializes in safe retirement planning and estate preservation. Some of Greg's professional designations include Certified Estate Planner (CEP®) and the esteemed Registered Financial Consultant (RFC®) designation through the International Association of Registered Financial Consultants (IARFC), a worldwide network of highly trained financial professionals. These designations required extensive study, passing comprehensive exams in areas of taxation, investments, insurance, estate, trust, and retirement planning, as well as annual continuing education requirements. Greg has been securities licensed for over 25 years. He is an Investment Advisor Representative (IAR) and an Independent Licensed Insurance Representative focusing on estate planning products.

He studied finance at Ohio University, completed the College of Financial Planners Advanced Estate Planning and Trust course, and has not stopped learning and innovating for the last thirty years. His reputation with his clients is that of a very engaged problem solver who cares about his clients.

Greg entered the financial services field in 1981, and in 1989 became a national sales director of a large national financial services company. In 1992 he and a partner formed the well-known firm First City Estate Planning, Inc., which concentrated on estate preservation and served all of Ohio and West Virginia and parts of Pennsylvania. In early 2002 Greg dissolved his ownership interest in First City Estate Planning, Inc. to form Gregory Gentry & Associates, LLC, Marietta, Ohio, a more personal, family estate planning practice of which he is president and CEO.

Greg is a regular information source for local news, radio stations, and newspapers, and after years of encouragement from his clients, he is excited to have author added to his list of accomplishments.

Greg has been very active with Boy Scouts of America for over 25 years and was a scoutmaster for over 13 years. He is a Council Distinguished Eagle Scout, has two Eagle Scout sons and a third son who is working on his Eagle Scout project. Greg and his wife, Amy, their five children and two grandchildren live in Marietta, Ohio.

Gregory Gentry & Associates, LLC
520 Virginia St.
Marietta, Ohio 45750
Phone 740-373-3500
www.gregorygentry.com

CLIENT DISCOVERY QUESTIONNAIRE

Client Discovery Information

Today's Date _____

Name _____

Social Security # _____

Home Address _____

_____

(H) Phone _____ (W) Phone _____

E-mail _____

Fax _____

Date of Birth _____

Married _____ Single _____ Divorced _____ Widowed _____

Name of Employer

_____

Business Address _____

_____

Occupation _____

U.S. Citizen? Yes _____ No _____

Covered by Social Security? Yes _____ No _____

SPOUSE

Name _____

Social Security # _____

Date of Birth _____

Name of Employer

_____

Business Address _____

_____

(W) Phone _____

Occupation _____

U.S. Citizen? Yes ____ No ____

Covered by Social Security? Yes ____ No ____

DEPENDENTS

Name	Date of Birth	Relationship
_____	_____	_____
_____	_____	_____
_____	_____	_____
_____	_____	_____

Will your parents likely need financial help in the future?

Yes ____ No ____

If yes, please explain:

_____

_____

_____

CHILDREN'S EDUCATION

Will you pay for your children's college education?

Yes _____ No _____ Undecided _____

Will you pay for postgraduate work?

Yes _____ No _____ Undecided _____

How much do you estimate college and/or postgraduate school will cost per child per year in today's dollars? $ _____

Any potential gifts planned? _____

Have assets been set aside to cover this cost? Yes _____ No _____

How Much? _____

INCOME

	Current Client	Spouse	Total
Annual	$ _____	_____	_____
Salary	$ _____	_____	_____
Investment	$ _____	_____	_____
Other	$ _____	_____	_____

Anticipated future income. Please explain.

_____

_____

_____

_____

FINANCIAL INFORMATION

Cash and Cash Equivalents:	Client	Spouse	Total
Checking Account(s)	$ _____	_____	_____
Savings Account(s)	$ _____	_____	_____
Money Market Funds	$ _____	_____	_____
Certificates of Deposit	$ _____	_____	_____
Annuities	$ _____	_____	_____
Other	$ _____	_____	_____

Please enclose statements

NONRETIREMENT INVESTMENTS: STOCKS, BONDS, MUTUAL FUNDS

Owner Description	# Shares	Cost Basis	Value
_____	_____	_____	_____
_____	_____	_____	_____
_____	_____	_____	_____
_____	_____	_____	_____
_____	_____	_____	_____
_____	_____	_____	_____

Please provide the appropriate brokerage or mutual fund statement(s)

RETIREMENT INVESTMENTS: VESTED AMOUNTS

Owner IRA/SEP	Pension/Profit Sharing/401(k) Contributions
_____	_____
_____	_____
_____	_____
_____	_____
_____	_____

Do you anticipate receiving a pension?

Yes _____ No _____ From whom? _____

At what age? _____ How much per month/year $_____

Will this inflate? Yes _____ No _____

Do you anticipate receiving a pension?

Yes _____ No _____ From whom? _____

At what age? _____ How much per month/year $_____

Will this inflate? Yes _____ No _____

Do you anticipate receiving a pension?

Yes _____ No _____ From whom? _____

At what age? _____ How much per month/year $_____

Will this inflate? Yes _____ No _____

RETIREMENT

Your expected retirement age _____

Spouse's expected retirement age _____

How much annual income (in today's $) will you want at retirement?
$ _____

Do you anticipate working after retirement? Yes __ No __
Est. earnings $_____

PERSONAL PROPERTY

Approximate Value	Client	Spouse	Total
Home Furnishings	$_____	_____	_____
Autos	$_____	_____	_____
Clothing, Furs	$_____	_____	_____
Jewelry, Silver, Antiques	$_____	_____	_____
Other, Special Items	$_____	_____	_____

PERSONAL REAL ESTATE

Market value of **Primary** Residence $_____

Original Cost $_____

Land

Original Mortgage $_____ Remaining Bal $_____

Int. Rate _____% Term ____ yrs. Monthly Pmt. $ _____

Owner(s) _____

Market value of **Secondary** Residence $_____

Original Cost $_____

Original Mortgage $_____ Remaining Bal $_____

Int. Rate _____% Term ____ yrs. Monthly Pmt. $ _____

Owner(s) _____

INVESTMENT REAL ESTATE

Address	Income	Market Value

LIABILITIES

Creditor	Total Amtount	Monthly Payments

RISK MANAGEMENT

Life Insurance:

Policy Owner Insured	Beneficiary	Company	Death Benefit
_____	_____	_____	_____
_____	_____	_____	_____
_____	_____	_____	_____
_____	_____	_____	_____
_____	_____	_____	_____
_____	_____	_____	_____

Survivor's Income:

How much annual income would your family need to maintain their standard of living if one spouse were to die?

_____

_____

After your children become financially independent, how much annual income would the surviving spouse need?

_____

_____

What purpose does your life insurance serve?

_____

_____

Homeowners Insurance:

Property	Coverage	Liability Amt.	Company Deductible
_____	_____	$_____	_____
_____	_____	$_____	_____

Health Insurance:

Type of Coverage	Deductible	Stop-Loss Limit	Coinsurance %	Company
_____	$_____	$_____	_____	_____
_____	$_____	$_____	_____	_____

Hospital expenses, surgical expenses, major medical, comprehensive major medical, Blue Cross/Blue Shield, HMO, PPO, point of service plan, Medicare supplement/Medigap, etc.

Disability Income Insurance:

Insured % of Income	Waiting Period	Benefit Period	Company
_____	_____	_____	_____
_____	_____	_____	_____

In the event of your long-term disability, how much annual income would your family need to maintain its present standard of living in today's dollars? $_____

Long-Term Care Insurance:

Insured Daily Benefits	Waiting Period	Benefit Period	Company
$_____	_____	_____	_____
$_____	_____	_____	_____

Other Insurance:

When were your various insurance policies last reviewed?

_____

Do you have personal excess liability coverage?

Yes ____ No ____

What is the amount of this coverage? _____

ESTATE PLANNING

Do you have a will?

Yes ____ No ____ Date _____

Does your spouse have a will?

Yes ____ No ____ Date _____

Do you have a trust?

Yes ____ No ____ Date _____

Does your spouse have a trust?

Yes ____ No ____ Date _____

Do you have a durable power of attorney?

Yes ____ No ____ Date _____

Does your spouse have a durable POA?

Yes ____ No ____ Date _____

Do you have a health care POA?

Yes ____ No ____ Date _____

Does your spouse have a health care POA?

Yes ____ No ____ Date _____

Date(s) any of these documents were last reviewed:

_____

Do you expect to receive any inheritances?

Yes ____ No ____

If yes, please state from whom, approximate amounts, and any other information that might be helpful.

_____

_____

_____

GIFTS

Donor	Date of Gift	Donee(s)	Value Gifted	Tax Paid
_____	_____	_____	$_____	$_____
_____	_____	_____	$_____	$_____

Do you and/or your spouse intend to establish/continue a gifting program?

Yes ____ No ____

If yes, please explain: _____

_____

OBJECTIVES

Present

Which of the following best describes your attitude toward your income needs?

_____My present income is adequate for my needs.

_____I need more current income.

_____I can forego current income to be better able to provide for future income needs.

Other issues. Please explain _____

_____

_____

_____

What are your financial goals? _____

_____

_____

_____

What steps are you willing to take to achieve these goals? _____

_____

_____

_____

Rank the following financial objectives in their order of importance to you *(1 = most important, 8 = least important)*:

__ Conserving capital for heirs   __ Reduce current income taxes

__ Growth of capital   __ Reduce estate taxes

__ Increase current income   __ Children's education

__ Retirement income   __ Other _____

What is your primary financial concern? _____

_____

_____

_____

Is there anything else we should know to help you plan your financial future? _____

_____

_____

_____

INVESTMENT TEMPERAMENT

___% Very conservative investments; capital conservation is most important.

___% Generally conservative investments; capital appreciation with relatively safe, high quality investments is most important.

___% Investments with moderate risk; capital growth is most important.

___% Investments with high risk; aggressive capital growth is most important.

___% Total 100%

Are there any particular investments for which you have either a preference or an objection? Please explain. _____

_____

_____

_____

_____

_____

_____

BUSINESS INTERESTS

Owner	Address	Estimated Market Value	Annual Income
_____	_____	$_____	$_____
_____	_____	$_____	$_____
_____	_____	$_____	$_____
_____	_____	$_____	$_____
_____	_____	$_____	$_____
_____	_____	$_____	$_____

What would happen to your business in the event of your disability or death? _____

_____

_____

_____

_____

Does a binding purchase agreement exist for the sale of an owner's interest upon disability or death?

Yes ____ No ____

If yes, how is it funded and for how much? _____

_____

_____

_____

_____

Is there anything else we should know in order to evaluate or better understand your situation? _____

_____

_____

Professional Advisors

Accountant/Firm

_____

Attorney/Firm

_____

Banker/Bank

_____

Insurance Agent(s)/Firm(s)

_____

Portfolio Manager(s)/Firm(s)

_____

Stockbroker/Firm

_____

Other Professional Advisors

_____

_____

_____

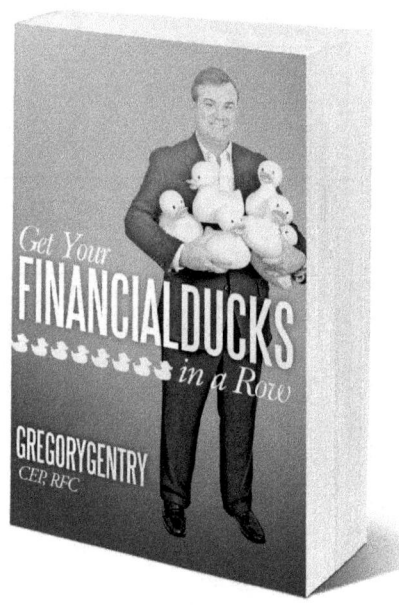

How can you use this book?

MOTIVATE

EDUCATE

THANK

INSPIRE

PROMOTE

CONNECT

Why have a custom version of *Get Your Financial Ducks in a Row?*

- Build personal bonds with customers, prospects, employees, donors, and key constituencies
- Develop a long-lasting reminder of your event, milestone, or celebration
- Provide a keepsake that inspires change in behavior and change in lives
- Deliver the ultimate "thank you" gift that remains on coffee tables and bookshelves
- Generate the "wow" factor

Books are thoughtful gifts that provide a genuine sentiment that other promotional items cannot express. They promote employee discussions and interaction, reinforce an event's meaning or location, and they make a lasting impression. Use your book to say "Thank You" and show people that you care.

Get Your Financial Ducks in a Row is available in bulk quantities and in customized versions at special discounts for corporate, institutional, and educational purposes. To learn more, please contact our Special Sales team at:

1.866.775.1696 • sales@advantageww.com • www.AdvantageSpecialSales.com